RISKY BUSINESS

Rodeo Clown

Laughs and Danger in the Ring

By

KEITH ELLIOT GREENBERG

With Photography by Bill Moyer

A BLACKBIRCH PRESS BOOK

WOODBRIDGE, CONNECTICUT

Published by Blackbirch Press, Inc.
One Bradley Road
Woodbridge, CT 06525

Printed in Hong Kong

10 9 8 7 6 5 4 3 2 1

Additional Photo Credits
Cover: ©Howell/Gamma-Liaison
Pages 14 and 15: ©Philippe Brylak/Gamma-Liaison

Library of Congress Cataloging-in-Publication Data

Greenberg, Keith Elliot.
    Rodeo clown/by Keith Greenberg.—1st ed.
      p.   cm. — (Risky business)
    Includes bibliographical reference and index.
    ISBN 1-56711-152-1 (lib. bdg.)
    1. Feller, Jim Bob—Juvenile literature. 2. Rodeo clowns—United
States—Biography—Juvenile literature. [1. Feller, Jim Bob. 2. Rodeo
clowns. 3. Clowns. 4. Rodeos.] I. Title. II. Series: Risky business
(Woodbridge, Conn.)
GV1833.6.F45G74   1995
791.8'4'092—dc20
[B]   94-39123
                                                  CIP
                                                     AC

When Jim Bob Feller turned seven, his grandfather gave him an unusual birthday present. It was a small woodcarving of a rodeo scene: a clown peeking out of a barrel, with charging bulls and bucking horses all around him.

No one at the time realized that Jim would eventually grow up to make a living this way.

For much of the year, the 43-year-old, easy-going Texan applies red and white grease paint to his face and slides himself into a barrel in the middle of a rodeo ring. At events around the United States, Jim and other rodeo clowns get in close, as a cowboy tries to stay on top of an angry bull for eight seconds. When the cowboy hits the dirt, it's the rodeo clown's job to distract the raging animal. While the cowboy scrambles to safety, a clown encourages the wild beast to charge the barrel, risking serious injury to himself at show after show.

As a rodeo clown, Jim Bob Feller dresses in a funny costume before each show.

A rodeo clown's life is full of close calls. Once, in Newport, Washington, a bull used its horns to spear off Jim Bob's clothes. Another time, in Thompson Falls, Montana, a bull actually fell on top of him. "All you could see were two arms, two feet, and my green hat," Jim remembers. "It's amazing that I had 1,800 pounds on me, and walked away without a scratch."

Scott Breding, a 32-year-old cowboy from Columbus, Montana, says, "Rodeo clowns protect us. The bull, by nature, follows movement when he's mad. He'd be following me if there were no rodeo clowns. Without them, there probably wouldn't be many bullriders around."

When a cowboy is thrown, it is the rodeo clown's job to get the animal's attention.

Jim still remembers the first time he saw a rodeo clown. It was at a rodeo in Waco, Texas. He marveled at the calf ropers, steer wrestlers, bullriders, and clowns he saw there. "I thought it was the biggest thing I'd ever seen in my life," he says.

Four years later, Jim was invited to be a part of a rodeo's "grand entry," where performers and locals parade around the arena on horseback. Eleven-year-old Jim rode on a horse with some members of his father's church. "I really thought I was Joe Cowboy then," he laughs.

Steer wrestling is one common part of a rodeo.

The "grand entry," with locals and performers on horseback, often begins a rodeo.

9

At age 13, Jim became a regular at the weekly Kowbell Rodeo in Mansfield, Texas. He was even introduced to Keith Anderson, a professional rodeo clown.

At 15, Jim felt he was athletic enough to become a rodeo clown. "I'm real fast," he told Keith Anderson. "I think I could be pretty good at this."

Keith replied that it took more than speed to be a rodeo clown. "You have to be able to run in circles and pivot to avoid the bull," he said.

Jim was not discouraged. He was certain that, sooner or later, he'd become a rodeo clown. What he had to decide was which type of rodeo clown he wanted to be: a bullfighter or barrel man.

A rodeo clown must be in excellent physical condition in order to run and pivot while being chased by a bull.

11

Inset: Barrel men try to get a bull to charge their barrel instead of a cowboy.

Bullfighter rodeo clowns get in close to a bull in order to get its attention.

12

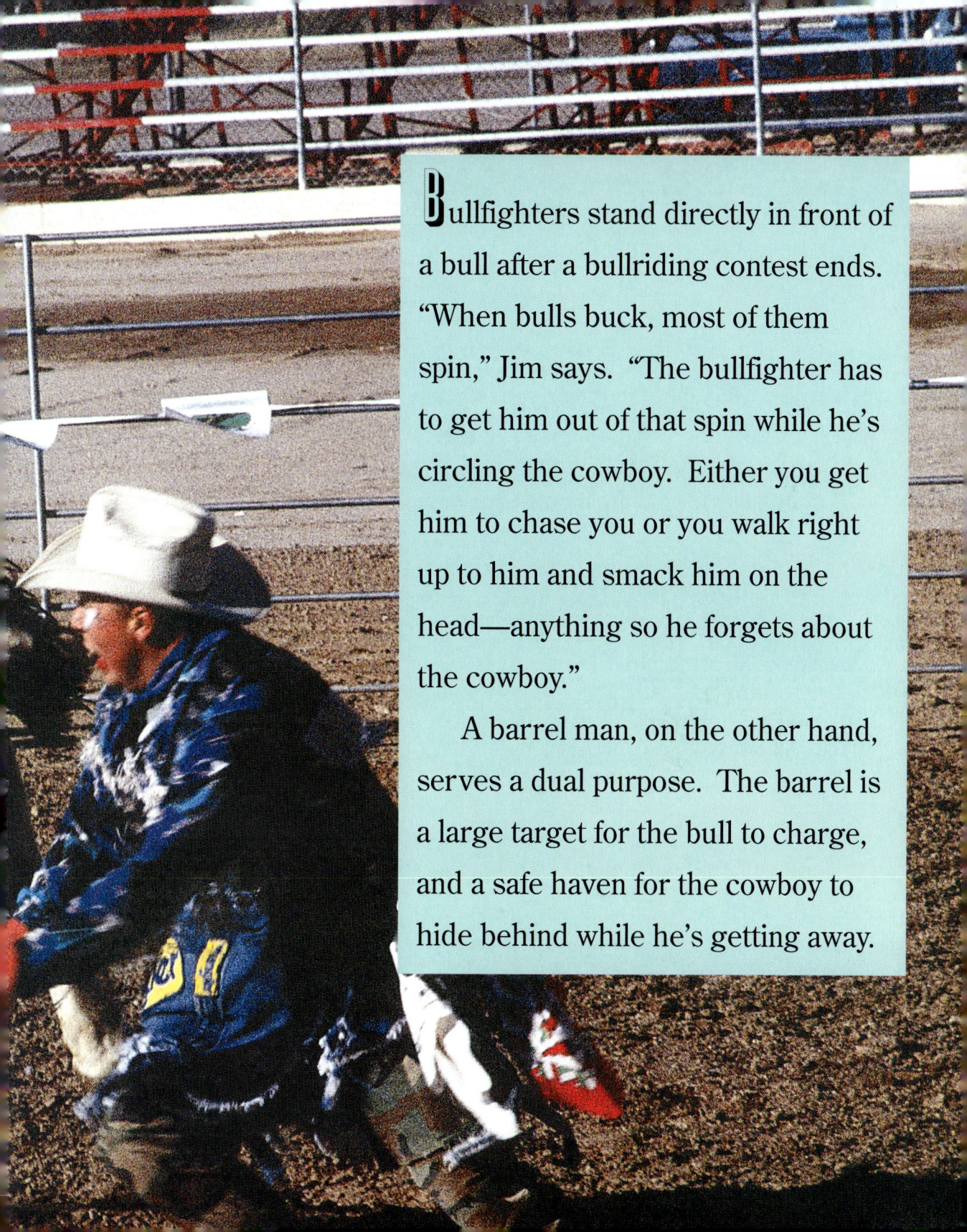

Bullfighters stand directly in front of a bull after a bullriding contest ends. "When bulls buck, most of them spin," Jim says. "The bullfighter has to get him out of that spin while he's circling the cowboy. Either you get him to chase you or you walk right up to him and smack him on the head—anything so he forgets about the cowboy."

A barrel man, on the other hand, serves a dual purpose. The barrel is a large target for the bull to charge, and a safe haven for the cowboy to hide behind while he's getting away.

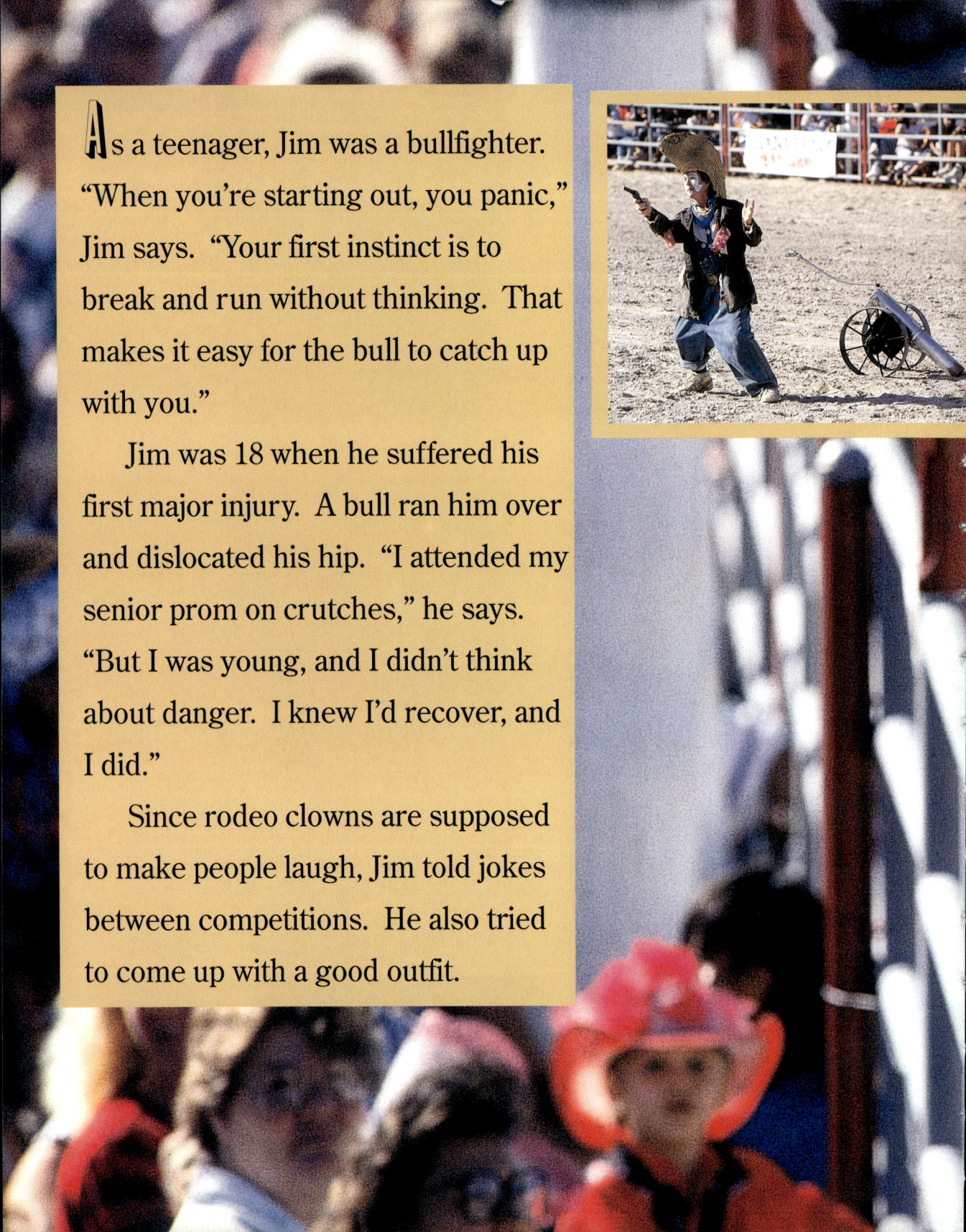

As a teenager, Jim was a bullfighter. "When you're starting out, you panic," Jim says. "Your first instinct is to break and run without thinking. That makes it easy for the bull to catch up with you."

Jim was 18 when he suffered his first major injury. A bull ran him over and dislocated his hip. "I attended my senior prom on crutches," he says. "But I was young, and I didn't think about danger. I knew I'd recover, and I did."

Since rodeo clowns are supposed to make people laugh, Jim told jokes between competitions. He also tried to come up with a good outfit.

Part of a rodeo clown's job is to make people laugh.

Inset: One clown does a comedy routine in between events.

15

16

Jim studies the bulls and horses
before each rodeo so he has an
idea of how each will react.

As a bullfighter, Jim went out of his way to distract the bulls quickly. This strategy saved many a cowboy. The bullriders realized that Jim was especially good and they began asking to work with him.

Jim always tried to study the bulls in their pens before each rodeo. First, he noted the breed—Brahma, Braford, Angus, Charolais, Beefmaster, or Mexican fighting bull. What kind of personality did it have? Would it charge at a clown immediately, or back away until pushed into a battle?

"You have to respect them," he explains. "If you don't, they're going to take you by surprise and zap you."

The only thing between a barrel man and an angry bull is a barrel.

In 1983, Jim became a barrel man. Even though he did not have to run around as much as a bullfighter, the chances of becoming seriously hurt were still great.

"A bull will hit that barrel every performance," Jim explains. "You take a pounding. Every day, you're sore. I've been hooked in the back. They've hit my ribs and my legs. I've had my head sewn up a couple of times. It's an art in itself to control that barrel and use it like a shield from the bull."

18

Jim speaks to some of his young fans during a personal appearance.

Despite the danger, only a handful of the clowns in the Professional Rodeo Cowboys Association (PRCA)—the largest rodeo organization in the United States—make a living solely from performing. Popular clowns are on the road constantly, appearing at between 20 and 30 rodeos annually. Each event is usually between three and four days long.

While cowboys compete for a cash prize—and the losers go home broke—clowns receive a fee from each rodeo. Some clowns get large companies to sponsor them. Jim's sponsor is American Home Foods. They pay him to promote their product, Ranch Style Beans, wherever he travels.

Jim signs autographs as he promotes the product of the company that sponsors him.

21

Performing in front of cheering crowds may seem like it's all fun. But family life is hard for a rodeo clown. Jim has missed his children's birthdays and family holidays because of his career.

The traveling and busy schedule can be almost as difficult as battling the bulls. Once, Jim worked at a rodeo in Kansas, then drove two and a half days to Washington State. After that rodeo, he drove back to Kansas, to an event just 15 miles from the first one. When he arrived, he found that the promoter had already hired another rodeo clown.

Life on the road can be hard for rodeo clowns with families at home.

Jim applies his special makeup in stages before each show.

Jim's trailer is full of props. Before performing, he puts together his gag explosives that will blow up when he drives his car around the arena.

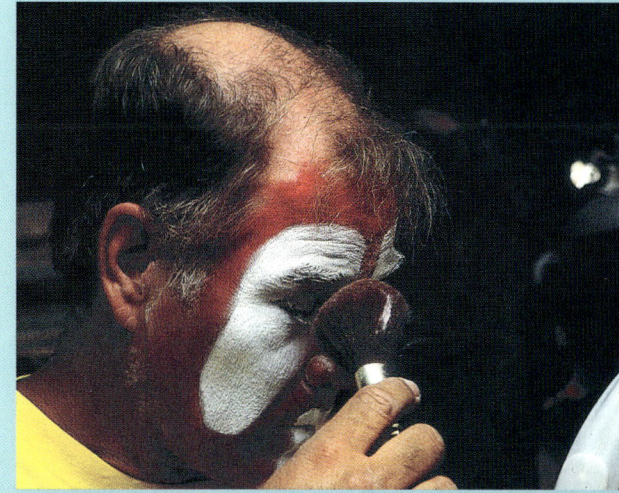

Shortly before a show, Jim gets into his outfit: a green hat, blond wig, baggy overalls, striped shirt, and yellow neckerchief. He also applies white grease paint to his mouth and eyes, covers the rest of his face in red, and

draws black designs over his cheeks and forehead. To prevent his makeup from running, he dabs his face with baby powder. "It's like you put on a suit and go to work," he jokes. "Just another day at the office."

Jim checks out the bulls before one rodeo in New Mexico. "Let's see who I'm fighting tonight," he says, looking through the railing at the bulls. "Oh, I recognize these guys. Some of these bulls have a set pattern. But when you start to think you know them, it backfires. That's when you get hurt."

Meanwhile, the cowboys are also preparing. Since their livelihood depends on whether they win or lose, the mood is tense. Behind the scenes, they stretch and twist their bodies, preparing to meet the bulls that will try to toss them. One man covers his face with his hat and prays.

One cowboy suits up outside before the show.

Cowboys prepare for their contests backstage before the rodeo.

27

As expected, a cowboy is hurled through the air soon after the rodeo starts. Jim quickly runs to the middle of the arena and tells the crowd, "These horses are sick to their stomachs. They're all throwing up cowboys."

The spectators chuckle, and Jim focuses on a bald man in the audience. "It's all off!" the clown shouts. "It's all off!"

"What's all off?" the crowd yells back.

"The hair on that man's head!"

A bucking bronco tosses off its rider as it jumps high in the air.

During the bullriding competition, one cowboy after another does his best to stay on a fierce, bucking bull. After each try, the bullfighting clowns steer the bull into a passage leading to an enclosed pen. One beast proves more stubborn than the rest. It rushes a barrel and knocks it over on its side.

As the crowd gasps, a clown's hand emerges, waving a white flag of surrender. The arena is filled with cheers. The rodeo clown has done his job.

Below: A bullfighter and a barrel man work together to get a bull's attention.

Bottom: Jim entertains the crowd with his exploding car.

FURTHER READING

Bellville, Cheryl W. *Rodeo*. Minneapolis, MN: Carolrhoda Books, 1985.

Fain, James W. *Rodeos*. Chicago: Childrens, 1987.

Martini, Teri. *Cowboys*. Chicago: Childrens, 1981.

Rice, James. *Cowboy Rodeo*. Gretna, LA: Pelican Publishing Company, 1992.

INDEX